That's My Name! Say It Right!

ADELA VILLALPANDO

GLOBAL
PUBLISHING
SOLUTIONS

THAT'S MY NAME! SAY IT RIGHT! by Adela Villalpando

Published by Global Publishing Solutions, LLC
923 Fieldside Drive
Matteson, Illinois 60443
www.globalpublishingsolutions.com

Illustrated by Rodolfo Villalpando

Library of Congress Control Number:
2023909031
International Standard Book Number:
979-8-9853892-6-5
E-book International Standard Book Number:
979-8-9853892-7-2

Printed in the United States of America

Dedication

First and foremost, praises and thanks to God for all the blessings he provides for us on a daily basis.

I would like to thank my husband, Manuel, for his support in helping me achieve my dream of writing this book. Thanks to my adult children, Melinda, Nicolas, Rodolfo, and Victor, who were also very supportive in the process of completing this book. My grandchildren Matthew and Christian also provided feedback on this book.

That's My Name!

Say It Right!

Antonio

Zacarias

Adela Villalpando and Rodolfo Villalpando

A

A is for Antonio

(An-to-nee-o)

Antonio likes apples.

B

B is for Bella

(Bell-uh)

Bella has a bike.

C

C is for Carlos

(Car-los)

Carlos will eat a cupcake.

D

D is for Daniel

(Dan-yel)

Daniel likes dinosaurs.

E

E is for Elena

(El-ay-nuh)

Elena is sitting next to an elephant.

F

F is for Fernando

(Fer-nan-do)

Fernando is playing football.

G

G is for Gabino

(Ga-bee-no)

Gabino is eating grapes.

H

H is for Hilda

(Hil-duh)

Hilda is washing her hands.

I

I is for Irma

(Er-muh)

Irma is eating an ice cream cone.

J

J is for Javier

(Hah-vee-air)

Javier is jumping rope.

K

K is for Katrina

(Ka-tree-nuh)

Katrina is flying a kite.

L

L is for Linda

(Lin-duh)

Linda loves lemons.

M

M is for Manuel

(Mahn-well)

Manuel has a map.

N

N is for Nicolas

(Ni-co-las)

Nicolas is taking a nap.

O

O is for Omar

(Oh-mar)

Omar saw an owl.

P

P is for Pedro

(Pe-dro)

Pedro is eating popcorn.

Q

Q is for Quiana

(Qui-a-nuh)

Quiana is very quiet.

R

R is for Rosa

(Ro-suh)

Rosa is pointing at the rainbow.

S

S is for Salvador

(Sal-vuh-dor)

Salvador made a sandcastle.

T

T is for Tomas

(Toe-mahs)

Tomas lost a tooth.

U

U is for Ulysses

(U-liss-ses)

Ulysses is on a unicorn.

V

V is for Victor

(Vic-ter)

Victor plays the violin.

W

W is for Wilfredo

(Wil-fre-do)

Wilfredo bought a new watch.

X

X is for Xavier

(X-aye-vee-er)

Xavier has a xylophone.

Y

Y is for Yadira

(Ya-dee-ruh)

Yadira has a yo-yo.

Z

Z is for Zacarias

(Za-cuh-rye-us)

Zacarias is at the zoo.

Most of us like to hear our name, so it is important to pronounce it correctly.

You can use the website to hear how a name is pronounced.

Some names are often used for both boys and girls. We just change (or add) a letter or two in their name.

Here are a few names that are used for boys and girls.

Boy	Girl
Tomas	Tomasa
Fernando	Fernanda
Gabriel	Gabriela
Manuel	Manuela
Victor	Victoria
Ramon	Ramona
Mario	Maria

And this is the end of That's My Name! Say It Right!

Illustrations by Rodolfo Villalpando

ABOUT THE AUTHOR

Adela Villalpando came from a family of ten. Because she was the secon oldest, she had to take care of all of her siblings. That is where her love for carin and nurturing children began.

Adela lives in a small town called Elsa, Texas. This little city is located in the Ri Grande Valley. She has lived there for most of her life. While she was growing u her family would migrate to California during the summer to work in the fields. few years later, after her high school graduation, she married her loving husban Manuel Villalpando.

The couple has been blessed with four children, Melinda, Nicolas, Rodolfo, an Victor. Adela has two grandchildren as well, named Matthew and Christian. Th family has tried to make time for each other, and they have created man memories over the years.

Adela has been associated with children throughout her life. She worked fo Head Start as a classroom teacher, center manager, disability coordinator, an family coordinator. She was also active in the community and taught bible classe to children for several years. Adela has always been intrigued with childre because they are so honest and funny.

She has been teaching pre-K and kindergarten for the past fourteen years a Monte Alto I.S.D.

Monte Alto is a very small community where everyone comes together to hel those who are in need of some sort of assistance.

It has been a dream for Adela to be an author, and her dream is becoming reality with this book. As an educator, she plans to continue writing books. Sh would like to inspire children and adults that they are capable of fulfilling thei dreams if they work hard at it.

Never give up on your dreams.